D0831221

The Art of
Parenting

by *Drew de Soto*

It's a balancing act

Shoulder
sick

0+

You promise yourself it will never happen

0+

They pee on you and think it's funny

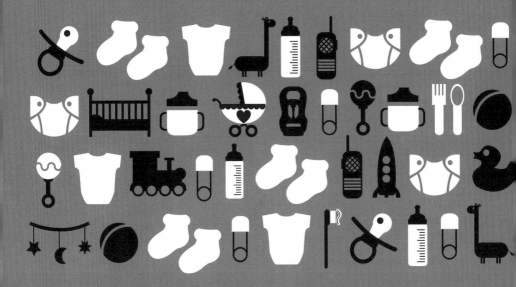

Overnight stay

Before and after

0+

Bath

0+

Before and after

0+

Major
hazard

"The wheels on the bus go round and round, round and round..."

Ad nauseam

Don't forget swimming nappies

Lose this and *you're* stuffed

Pacifier

Roadside
WC

2+

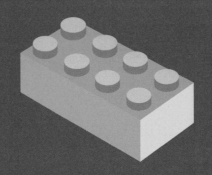

Unimaginable pain

Sometimes
Always
Never

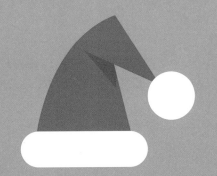

The enforcer

Weapon of mass destruction

Negotiating tools

Stereotypes
will apply

Play date

Their idea, your idea

3+

Why? Why?
Why? Why?
Why? Why?
Why? Why?
Why?..

"What do you want to eat?" "Nothing."

3+

Instant playback

You should buy shares in these

Sometimes
Always
Never

Anxiety making but, A to B enabling

SKIP

Your car

3+

Happy torture

They go along with it for the money

Next time just buy the box

At the end of the day, we're all just winging it

From start to finish

Original content: Fitzroy de Soto
Additional contributions by: Bee de Soto
Illustrated by: Drew de Soto, Cris Convery and Ben Midson

B*IS*

BIS Publishers
Building Het Sieraad
Postjesweg 1
1057 DT Amsterdam
The Netherlands
T (31) 020 515 02 30
bis@bispublishers.com
www.bispublishers.com

ISBN 978-90-6369-480-7

Copyright © 2018 Drew de Soto and BIS Publishers

All rights reserved. No part of this publication may be
reproduced or transmitted in any form or by any means,
electronic or mechanical, including photocopy, recording
or any information storage and retrieval system, without
permission in writing from the copyright owners.

Design by Navig8 www.navig8.co.uk
Visit www.theartofparenting.co.uk